Tastes&Flavors
of **PINEAPPLE**

Tastes&Flavors
of **PINEAPPLE**

Muriel Miura

MUTUAL PUBLISHING

Library of Congress Cataloging-in-Publication Data

Miura, Muriel.
    Tastes & flavors of pineapple / Muriel Miura.
        p. cm.
    Summary: "A collection of recipes ranging from appetizer to dessert that uses
    pineapple as an essential ingredient"--Provided by publisher.
    ISBN-13: 978-1-56647-819-9 (hardcover : alk. paper)
    ISBN-10: 1-56647-819-7 (hardcover : alk. paper)
    1. Cookery (Pineapples) I. Title. II. Title: Tastes and flavors of pineapple.
    TX813.P5M58 2006
    664'.072--dc22

                        2006034215
ISBN-10: 1-56647-819-7
ISBN-13: 978-1-56647-819-9

Illustrations by Jenny Nakai
Photographs on pages 1, 3, 9, 21, 28, 37, 48, 57, 60, 65, 72, & 75 © Douglas Peebles
All other photographs by Ray Wong
Design by Emily R. Lee

First Printing, April 2007
1 2 3 4 5 6 7 8 9

Mutual Publishing, LLC
1215 Center Street, Suite 210
Honolulu, Hawai'i 96816
Ph: 808-732-1709 / Fax: 808-734-4094
E-mail: info@mutualpublishing.com
www.mutualpublishing.com

Printed in Korea

Table of Contents

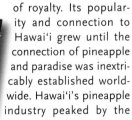

Introduction

The pineapple, long reigning as the king of fruits, is a native of South America and was a favorite luxury of privileged Europeans as far back as the fifteenth century. It is believed that Spaniards introduced pineapple to Hawai'i in the sixteenth century when they unintentionally arrived on the Big Island on their way back from Mexico. Although it is not a native crop, the pineapple eventually made a home in Hawai'i, where the year-round sunny climate and tropical rains and rich volcanic soil produced the finest pineapple in the world.

In the twentieth century, pineapple flourished in Hawai'i, marking an era of hospitality and agricultural success in the islands. Its exotic, sweet flavor and versatility for cooking delighted visitors and residents alike. Pineapple became a marketing logo for the tourism industry, luring many to drink cocktails on the beach and, of course, to buy Hawaiian pineapple. Promoted as superior to varieties grown elsewhere, Hawai'i's pineapple was produced predominantly by Dole, Del Monte, and Libby.

Images of paradise featuring the pineapple were embellished with other familiar icons such as the hula girl, flower lei, palm trees, even the 'ukulele. Topped with its own crown, the fruit naturally inspired a metaphor of royalty. Its popularity and connection to Hawai'i grew until the connection of pineapple and paradise was inextricably established worldwide. Hawai'i's pineapple industry peaked by the

mid-1950s, when it produced almost 75 percent of the world's pineapple supply.

Hawai'i enjoyed its pineapple boom until the turn of the millennium, when sadly, the industry experienced its demise as the major labels sought overseas cultivation in the Philippines, Thailand, even Mexico to benefit from lower production costs. Today, Hawai'i produces less than two percent of the global market, most of which stem from O'ahu's remnant fields and Maui. Lāna'i, once known as the Pineapple Isle, still grows about 100 acres but only for local consumption. With the symbolic Dole Pineapple water tower gone, the cannery in Iwilei converted to movie theaters, and former fields lying fallow or taken over by other development projects, what remains of the pineapple era on O'ahu is the Dole Plantation in Wahiawā.

Though the reign of pineapple in Hawai'i seems over, the memories of its glory days and past prosperity still linger sweetly. Even now, whenever anyone sees a pineapple or enjoys its tantalizing, fresh flavor, one cannot help thinking of Hawai'i.

APPETIZERS & SALADS

Seafood Cocktail

Serves 6

A simple seafood cocktail enhanced by pineapple chunks.

1 can (1-1/4 pounds) pineapple chunks, drained
1/2 pound fresh shrimp or crabmeat, cooked
Seafood cocktail (purchased)
Lettuce, washed and patted dry
Chives, chopped

Toss pineapple chunks with shrimp or crabmeat and cocktail sauce to taste. Chill. Spoon into lettuce-lined cocktail glasses and sprinkle with chives to serve.

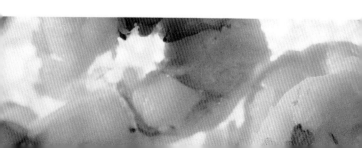

Mango Chutney-Cheese Pâté

Makes about 4 cups

The exotic flavors of pineapple and mango are a nice mix for this pâté.

1 package (8 ounces) cream cheese, unwrapped
1 can (1-1/4 pounds) crushed pineapple, drained well
1 cup mango chutney
Wheat Thins or sesame crackers

Place block of cream cheese on large wooden serving tray; set aside. Combine pineapple with chutney; mix until well blended and spoon over cream cheese. Surround with crackers to serve.

Baked Spring Rolls

Makes 72 pieces

These spring rolls are less in calories as they're baked, not fried.

Filling:
1 can (1-1/4 pounds) crushed pineapple, drained
1 can (4 ounces) water chestnuts, drained and diced
1/4 cup chopped green onion
1 package (12 ounces) bean sprouts, blanched and drained
2 cans (4 ounces) deveined shrimp
3/4 pound fresh cooked shrimp, deveined and shelled

2 cans (8 ounces) refrigerated crescent rolls
1 egg, beaten
Soy sauce

Combine pineapple, water chestnuts, onions, and bean sprouts. Chop and fold in shrimp. Open one can refrigerated rolls; unroll dough and separate into 4 rectangles and pinch together diagonal separations. Roll each rectangle on lightly floured surface to 7 × 9 inches. Cut each rectangle into 3 strips, 7 × 3 inches each. Spoon one heaping tablespoon of Filling into center of each strip, spreading lengthwise. Moisten edges with water; roll dough over Filling lengthwise. Press open ends with tines of fork to seal. Place on lightly greased baking sheet and brush with beaten egg. Repeat with second can of rolls. Bake at 375°F for 25 to 30 minutes or until golden brown. Slice each diagonally with serrated knife into 3 bite-size rolls. Serve hot with soy sauce as dip, if desired.

Bleu Cheese Dip

Makes about 2 cups

*The perfect dip for crudités—cold, crisp cucumbers,
broccoli, celery, and more!*

1 package (8 ounces) cream cheese, softened
1 package (4 ounces) bleu cheese, softened
1 tablespoon snipped chives
1/2 teaspoon dill weed
1 teaspoon seasoned salt
1/4 teaspoon garlic powder
1 can (8-1/4 ounces) crushed pineapple
Fresh raw vegetables of choice (celery, carrots, broccoli, cauliflower, cucumber, etc.)

Beat cream cheese and bleu cheese together until light and
fluffy. Beat in chives, dill weed, seasoned salt, and garlic
powder until well blended. Fold in pineapple and all syrup.
Chill 1 to 2 hours before serving with crudités.

TIP

To double a recipe, use twice the amount of each
ingredient. If possible, salt, pepper, and spices should
not be doubled without tasting first.

Koala Avocado

Serves 4

A nice combination of tuna with island fruits and nuts.

1 can (6-1/2 ounces) tuna, drained and flaked
2 tablespoons lemon juice
1 cup fresh or canned pineapple, cubed and drained
1/4 cup diced celery
1/4 cup macadamia nut bits
1/4 teaspoon salt
1/3 cup mayonnaise
1 tablespoon pineapple juice
2 medium ripe avocadoes, cut in half and brushed with
    lemon juice

Combine tuna, lemon juice, pineapple, celery, nuts, and salt.
Combine mayonnaise with pineapple juice and toss with tuna
mixture. Fill avocado halves with salad mixture. Place in oven
broiler; broil 5 to 6 minutes or until bubbly and light brown. If
desired, serve on bed of lettuce.

Hawaiian Star Salad

Serves about 6

This "starry" salad will make a hit with adults as well as keiki.

2 large firm-ripe papayas

Filling:
1/2 cup creamed cottage cheese
3 tablespoons cream cheese
1/8 teaspoon salt
1 tablespoon lemon juice
3/4 cup crushed pineapple, drained
Crisp lettuce leaves, washed and patted dry

Cut off stem end of papayas about one-fourth of the way down. Carefully scoop out seeds, retaining "star" shape in the center. Combine Filling ingredients in a bowl; mix until smooth. Pack cheese mixture into papayas; chill 1 to 2 hours. Cut crosswise in 1-inch slices and serve on bed of lettuce.

Chicken Chutney Salad

Serves about 6

This is an elegant salad to make ahead, especially for a ladies' get-together.

1 can (1-1/4 pounds) pineapple chunks, drained
2 tablespoons minced onion
2 cups diced cooked chicken
1 cucumber, coarsely chopped
1/2 cup chopped salad cashews
1 cup mayonnaise
2 tablespoons chutney
3/4 teaspoon seasoned salt
Crisp lettuce leaves, washed and patted dry

Combine onion, chicken, cucumber, cashews, and pineapple chunks in large bowl.; mix well. In separate bowl, combine mayonnaise, chutney, and seasoned salt; pour over chicken mixture and toss gently to mix well. Chill. Spoon chicken mixture onto bed of lettuce to serve.

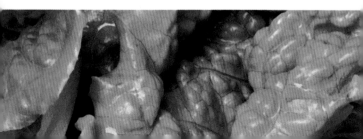

Calabash Salad

Serves 6–8

Nothing like a simple but delicious salad—easy to make, too!

1 medium head cabbage
1 cup fresh pineapple, drained and diced
1/4 teaspoon salt
1 cup shredded coconut
1-1/2 cups miniature marshmallows
1 cup whipping cream, whipped

Wash cabbage and remove outer leaves. Hollow out center leaving 1-inch thickness around edge. Shred about two cups of cabbage removed from center; combine with pineapple, salt, coconut, and marshmallows. Fold cabbage mixture into whipped cream and spoon into cabbage bowl. Chill and serve.

Seafoam Salad

Serves about 8

A refreshing, pale green froth with a delicate flavor.

1 can (1-1/4 pounds) crushed pineapple
1 package (6 ounces) lime gelatin
1 cup water
1/4 teaspoon seasoned salt
1/4 teaspoon dill weed
1/4 cup dry vermouth, optional
2 cups dairy sour cream
Crisp salad greens, washed

Drain pineapple well; reserve all syrup. Add syrup to gelatin in 2-quart saucepan. Stir in water, salt, and dill weed; heat to boiling, stirring constantly, until gelatin dissolves. Remove from heat; stir in vermouth, if used. Chill until mixture reaches consistency of unbeaten egg white. Blend in sour cream; fold in pineapple. Pour mixture into 1-1/2-quart ring mold. Chill until firm. Unmold onto bed of salad greens to serve.

Pineapple-Crab Salad

Serves about 6

*The combination of pineapple and crabmeat
makes for an interesting flavor.*

2-1/2 cups diced fresh pineapple, chilled
1-1/2 cups shredded crabmeat
1 tablespoon tomato catsup
1/2 teaspoon Worcestershire sauce, optional
1/3 cup mayonnaise
Crisp lettuce leaves, washed and patted dry

Mix together chilled pineapple and crabmeat; place on bed
of lettuce. Combine catsup, Worcestershire sauce, and mayonnaise; mix well and pour over salad to serve.

Hawaiian Ambrosia

Serves about 6

A refreshing combination of tropical fruits.

2 cups fresh pineapple cubes
1 cup diced firm-ripe papaya
1/2 cup maraschino cherries or Surinam cherries
16 to 20 miniature marshmallows, optional
1 large banana, sliced
3/4 cup fresh grated coconut

Combine pineapple, papaya, cherries, and marshmallows; chill.
Just before serving, add bananas and coconut; toss lightly to
combine. Serve as dessert in sherbet glass or pineapple shell.

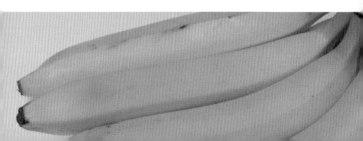

ENTREÉS

Pineapple-Beef Kabobs

Serves about 6

These kabobs are popular at any party—try them!

Marinade:
1/2 cup soy sauce
2 tablespoons canola oil
1/4 cup sugar
1 teaspoon minced fresh ginger root
1 clove garlic, crushed

2 pounds top sirloin beef*, cut into 1-inch cubes
18 mushrooms, cleaned
18 cherry tomatoes
1 can (8-1/4 ounces) pineapple chunks, drained
1 green pepper, cubed

Combine Marinade ingredients in a ziplock plastic bag and shake to combine well; marinate beef in bag at least 1 hour. Thread marinated meat, mushroom, tomato, pineapple, and green pepper alternately on wooden skewers that have been soaked in water for 1 hour. Place kabobs on broiler pan rack to cook. Broil about 3 inches from heat 8 to 10 minutes; turn and baste with Marinade. Broil additional 8 to 10 minutes or until meat is cooked to desired doneness.

*Chicken may be substituted for beef.

Pineapple Lobster with Black Beans

Serves about 4

Chinese black beans and pineapple uniquely flavor this lobster dish.

2 lobster tails
1-1/2 tablespoons canola oil
1 clove garlic, crushed
2 teaspoons Chinese black beans, crushed
1 slice fresh ginger, crushed

Sauce:
2 tablespoons soy sauce
1 teaspoon sugar
1 teaspoon cornstarch
2 tablespoons water
1 teaspoon sherry
1 teaspoon minced green onion
1/2 cup pineapple chunks

Chinese parsley for garnish

Cut lobster tails into 1-inch pieces. Sauté garlic in hot canola oil 1 minute, then stir-fry lobster for 5 minutes. Add crushed black beans with crushed ginger. Stir-fry one minute, then add the combined Sauce ingredients and cook over low heat until slightly thickened; cover and simmer about 5 minutes. Add pineapple chunks. Garnish with Chinese parsley and serve with hot steamed rice.

Pineapple Meat Rings

Serves 10

Another way to serve hamburger meat.

1 pound ground beef
1/2 cup bread crumbs
1 egg, beaten
1 cup milk
1-1/4 teaspoons salt
1/4 cup minced onion
1/8 teaspoon black pepper
1/4 teaspoon dry mustard
Dash sage
1 teaspoon curry
10 pineapple slices

Parsley and stuffed olive for garnish

Combine all ingredients except pineapple slices; mix well. Shape meat mixture like a doughnut and place on individual pineapple slices. Place on rack in baking pan. Bake at 350°F for 45 minutes. Garnish with parsley and stuffed olive in center of each pineapple slice.

Oven-Braised Short Ribs

Serves about 6

Scrumptious, meaty short ribs oven braised in a tangy mustard sauce are bound to be a family favorite.

4 pounds short ribs, cut into serving-size pieces
1 can (1-1/4 pounds) pineapple chunks, drained, reserving syrup
1/4 cup Dijon mustard
1/2 cup chopped onion
2 tablespoons soy sauce
1 teaspoon thyme, crushed
1/4 teaspoon garlic powder
1/4 cup dry sherry
1 tablespoon cornstarch
1/4 cup chopped green onions

Place ribs fat side up in shallow roasting pan lined with aluminum foil. Blend 1/2 cup pineapple syrup, mustard, onion, soy sauce, thyme, and garlic powder; pour over ribs. Bake at 350°F for 2-1/2 hours or until tender. Remove short ribs to serving platter. Blend remaining pineapple syrup, sherry, and cornstarch; stir into pan juices until thickened and clear. Stir in pineapple chunks and green onions until heated through. Spoon over short ribs and serve with hot, steamed rice.

Aloha Chicken

Serves 4

The delicate flavor of chicken is enhanced with a delicious pineapple sauce.

Pineapple Sauce:

1/2 cup butter or margarine
1 teaspoon cornstarch
1 teaspoon lemon zest
1/4 cup fresh lemon juice
2/3 cup crushed pineapple with syrup
2 tablespoons minced onion
1 teaspoon soy sauce
1/4 teaspoon powdered thyme, optional

2 ready-to-cook young chickens (about 4 pounds), split in half
Four 6- to 8-inch skewers
1/2 teaspoon salt
1/4 teaspoon pepper
1/2 cup melted butter or margarine
1 can pineapple rings, drained
1/2 firm-ripe papaya, cut in eighths

To prepare Pineapple Sauce, melt butter or margarine in saucepan over low heat. Blend in cornstarch and stir in remaining ingredients; mix well. Cook 5 minutes. Set aside.

To prepare chicken, skewer leg and wing to body to make chicken half compact and flat; sprinkle with salt and pepper. Place on broiler grid and brush with melted butter or margarine. Broil 5 to 7 inches from heat. Turn over two or three times while broiling; baste with melted butter or margarine each time. Broil 25 to 40 minutes or until done. After 5 minutes before the end of cooking time, place pineapple rings and papaya slices on broiler grid; brush chicken and fruits with Pineapple Sauce. Garnish with parsley, if desired.

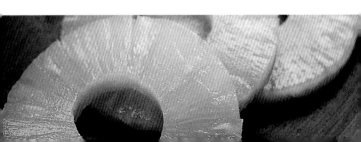

Sweet and Sour Spareribs

Serves about 6

A combination that can't be beat—batter-coated fried pork pieces with vegetables and pineapple.

2 pounds spareribs, cut in 1-1/2-inch pieces
2 teaspoons salt
1 teaspoon sherry
2 teaspoons soy sauce
1/4 cup cornstarch
3 tablespoons salad oil

Sauce:
1/2 cup brown sugar, packed
2/3 cup cider vinegar
2 tablespoons soy sauce
2 tablespoons tomato catsup
1/2 cup pineapple syrup (saved from canned pineapple chunks)
3 teaspoons cornstarch

1 large firm-ripe tomato, wedged
1 large sweet onion, wedged
1 medium green pepper, wedged
1 can (8 ounces) pineapple chunks, drained

In a small bowl, mix together spareribs, salt, sherry, soy sauce, and cornstarch; let stand 15 to 20 minutes. Heat oil in skillet and brown pork until golden; cover and simmer over medium heat 15 minutes. Drain excess fat. Stir in Sauce ingredients; bring to a boil. Add tomato wedges, onion, green pepper, and pineapple; cook additional minute. Serve with hot steamed rice immediately.

Baked Pineapple Ham

Serves 8–10

*Everyone enjoys baked ham with a tangy
pineapple glaze during the holidays—here's an
easy recipe to sparkle your holiday table.*

1 (8-pound) bone-in fully cooked smoked ham
1 can (1-1/4 pounds) sliced pineapple, drained,
    reserving syrup
1 cup apricot preserves
1 teaspoon dry mustard
Whole cloves
Maraschino cherries

Remove rind from ham; place fat side up on rack in roasting
pan. Insert meat thermometer with bulb centered in thickest
part of meat but not touching fat. Bake at 325°F for 18 to
20 minutes per pound for fully cooked ham or until thermometer registers 140°F*.

Meanwhile, combine reserved syrup with apricot preserves
and mustard for glaze; cook to reduce by half. Remove ham
from oven 30 minutes before done. Using toothpicks, skewer
pineapple slices over entire ham surface; stud with cloves.

Place a cherry in center of each pineapple slice; secure with toothpick. Brush with glaze and return to oven. Continue brushing with glaze every 10 minutes until done.

*Temperature of ham can be checked with instant read thermometer instead, thereby eliminating the insertion of thermometer into the ham during baking. Follow manufacturer's instructions regarding use of thermometer.

Glazed Pork Chops

Serves about 6

*The subtle flavors of the Orient blend nicely to
make a delicious glaze sauce.*

6 large pork chops
2 teaspoons salt
1/4 teaspoon ground ginger
1 (1-1/4 pounds) pineapple slices, drained, reserving all syrup
1/2 cup plum jam
1/4 cup chopped green onion

Cut a piece of fat from the pork chops and render in skillet.
Brown chops well on both sides. Sprinkle with salt and
ginger. Blend syrup and jam; pour over pork chops. Cover and
simmer 30 minutes. Add pineapple slices and green onions;
spoon pan juices over to heat pineapples. Serve with hot,
steamed rice.

Zesty Sausage Meatloaf

Serves 6–8

*Everyone enjoys meatloaf, and it's even more delicious with
sausage adding a new dimension of flavor and texture.*

1 pound ground sausage
2 pounds lean ground beef
1 can (13-1/4 ounces) crushed pineapple
1/2 cup fine dry bread crumbs
1/2 cup smoky barbecue sauce
1/2 cup minced onion
1 tablespoon chopped parsley
1 egg, slightly beaten
2 teaspoons horseradish
1/2 teaspoon garlic powder

Combine sausage and ground beef; mix thoroughly. Blend in
pineapple and all syrup, bread crumbs, barbecue sauce, onion,
parsley, egg, horseradish, and garlic powder. Form into a loaf
in a 9 × 12-inch baking pan. Bake at 350°F for 1 to 1-1/2 hours
or until done.

Sweet-Sour Fish

Serves about 4

Deliciously seasoned, delicately flavored fish is moist and juicy
when cooked this way and the presentation, unique.

1 whole (2 to 2-1/2 pounds) fish (uhu, 'ōpakapaka, ehu), scaled
    and cleaned
Flour
Oil for deep-frying

Sweet-Sour Sauce:
1/2 cup brown sugar, packed
2/3 cup vinegar
2 tablespoons soy sauce
3 tablespoons catsup
1/2 cup pineapple syrup
1 tablespoon cornstarch

1 large tomato, wedged
1 large onion, sliced
1 medium green pepper, wedged
1 can pineapple chunks, drained, reserving syrup
Chinese parsley (cilantro)

Cut 2 to 3 diagonal slits on each side of fish; dredge with flour. Fry in oil heated to 365°F to 375°F for 1 to 2 minutes on each side until golden brown, spooning hot oil over fish while frying. Drain on absorbent paper.

Combine Sweet-Sour Sauce ingredients in saucepan; bring to a boil. Add tomato, onion, green pepper, and pineapple; cook additional minute. Pour over cooked fish; sprinkle Chinese parsley over and serve immediately.

Hawaiian Bean Bake

Serves about 4

Baked beans go well with hot dogs, leftover ham strips, and even Portuguese sausage.

2 cups cooked ham strips
2 tablespoons canola oil
1 can (1-3/4 pounds) baked beans
1/2 cup smokey barbecue sauce
1 large bell pepper, chopped
1/2 cup chopped onion
1 can (1-1/4 pounds) crushed pineapple, drained

Sauté ham in oil until browned in an ovenproof skillet. Combine beans, barbecue sauce, bell pepper, onion, and pineapple; stir into skillet. Bake at 350°F for 20 minutes or until flavors are blended and beans are bubbly. Great with hot, steamed rice or crackers.

NOTE

Hot dogs or Portuguese sausage may be substituted for the ham strips.

SWEETS & TREATS

Pineapple Upside Down Cake

Serves 8–10

Just like the one Grandma used to bake, only faster and easier.

2/3 cup butter
2/3 cup brown sugar, packed
1 can (1-1/4 pounds) sliced pineapple, drained, reserving syrup
9 maraschino cherries
1 package (18-1/4 ounces) yellow cake mix
1 cup water
1/3 cup pineapple syrup
1/3 cup canola oil
3 eggs, slightly beaten

Melt butter in 10-inch skillet with ovenproof handle. Add brown sugar and stir until well blended. Arrange pineapple slices close together in butter-sugar mixture. Cut extra slices into wedges and place between slices. Place a cherry in center of each slice; set aside. Blend cake mix with water, pineapple syrup, oil, and eggs in large mixer bowl; mix at low speed until moistened, about 30 seconds, then at medium speed for 1 to 2 minutes or until batter is smooth. Pour batter over pineapple in skillet. Bake at 350°F for 30 to 35 minutes or until cake is done. Let stand 5 to 10 minutes, then invert onto serving plate. Allow skillet to rest over cake a minute for syrup to drain. Serve warm or cold.

Pineapple Nut Bread

Makes 1 loaf

No need to butter this one! It is moist, delicious, and keeps well.

1-3/4 cups flour
2 teaspoons baking powder
1/4 teaspoon baking soda
1/2 teaspoon salt
3/4 cup chopped macadamia nuts
3/4 cup brown sugar, packed
3 tablespoons butter or margarine, softened
2 eggs, slightly beaten
1 cup crushed pineapple (do not drain)

Topping:
2 tablespoons sugar
1/2 teaspoon ground cinnamon

Mix together flour, baking powder, baking soda, and salt; add macadamia nuts and mix well. In a separate bowl, cream brown sugar, butter, and eggs until light and fluffy. Stir in half the flour and nut mixture and then the pineapple. Blend in remaining flour and nut mixture; pour into greased 9 × 5 × 3-inch loaf pan. Combine Topping ingredients and sprinkle over top. Bake at 350°F for 45 to 50 minutes or until wooden pick inserted comes out clean.

Lime Pineapple Pie

Serves 8–10

The combination of lime and pineapple is yummy and refreshing.

1 (9-inch) graham cracker pie shell
1-1/4 cups pineapple syrup and water
1 package (3 ounces) lime gelatin
1 pint vanilla ice cream, softened
1 can crushed pineapple, drained, reserving syrup
1 lime, sliced

Combine pineapple syrup and water in 2-quart saucepan to make 1-1/4 cups; heat to boiling over high heat and add gelatin. Stir until gelatin dissolves. Add ice cream and stir until melted smooth; place in refrigerator and chill 25 to 35 minutes or until mixture mounds when dropped from spoon. Fold in 1 cup crushed pineapple, reserving remainder; pour into pie shell. Chill 35 to 45 minutes or until firm and set. Garnish with remaining crushed pineapple and lime slices.

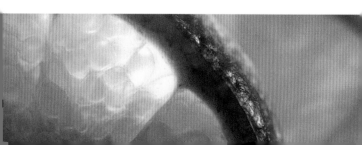

Pineapple Date Bars

Makes about 4 dozen

The perfect snack or dessert highlighting Hawai'i's "king of fruits."

1/3 cup butter or margarine, softened
2/3 cup brown sugar, packed
1/3 cup sugar
1/2 teaspoon baking soda
1-1/2 cups flour
Dash of salt
1 egg, slightly beaten
1 cup crushed pineapple, drained
2 cups dates, chopped fine
1/2 cup chopped macadamia nuts

Cream butter or margarine until fluffy. Add sugars, baking soda, flour, and salt; mix well. Stir in egg and crushed pineapple; add dates and nuts, mixing thoroughly. Spread in greased 8 × 12 × 2-inch pan. Bake at 350°F for 30 to 35 minutes or until golden brown. Cut into bars while still warm. Let cool in pan.

VARIATION

Drop from teaspoon onto greased baking sheet and bake 20 to 25 minutes for drop cookies.

Cocoa Pecan Pineapple Cookies

Makes about 4 dozen

A great item for the cookie jar and for nibbling any time.

1 cup butter or margarine, softened
1-1/2 cups brown sugar, packed
1 egg, slightly beaten
1 can (8-1/4 ounces) crushed pineapple
3-1/2 cups flour
3 tablespoons unsweetened cocoa
1 teaspoon baking powder
1 teaspoon ground cinnamon
1/2 teaspoon salt
1/2 cup chopped nuts (pecans, macadamia, almonds)

Cream butter until light. Beat in sugar until fluffy. Beat in egg until well blended, then fold in pineapple and all syrup. Combine flour, cocoa, baking powder, cinnamon, and salt; stir into pineapple mixture, then fold in nuts. Drop teaspoonfuls onto lightly greased baking sheets. Bake at 375°F for 12 to 15 minutes or until light brown around edges. Cool. Store in airtight container.

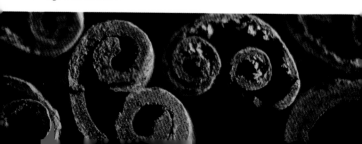

Pineapple Soufflé

Serves 6–8

A great tasting fluff of pineapple, cream, and Grand Marnier.

1 can (13-1/4 ounces) crushed pineapple
1 envelope unflavored gelatin
4 eggs, separated
1/4 cup Grand Marnier
1/4 teaspoon salt
1/3 cup sugar
1 cup whipping cream

Turn pineapple and all syrup into top of double boiler; sprinkle gelatin over surface and let stand 3 to 5 minutes to soften gelatin; set over boiling water. Beat egg yolks lightly and stir into pineapple. Cook, stirring constantly, until mixture coats spoon and gelatin is completely dissolved. Remove from heat and cool. Stir in Grand Marnier. Cool in refrigerator until mixture begins to thicken. Beat egg whites with salt to soft peaks. Gradually beat in sugar, beating until stiff peaks form. With same beater, whip cream stiff. Fold meringue and cream into cooled gelatin mixture; pour into 6-cup soufflé dish; chill until firm.

Mai Tai Pie

Serves 8–10

*The flavors of lime, pineapple, and rum are
distinctive in this coconut crust.*

Coconut Crust:
2 cups flaked coconut
1/4 cup butter, melted

Filling:
1 can (1-1/4 pounds) crushed pineapple, drained, reserving
    syrup
Water
2 envelopes unflavored gelatin
1/2 cup sugar
1/2 teaspoon salt
1 teaspoon lime zest
1 tablespoon fresh lime juice
3 eggs, separated
1/4 cup dark Jamaican rum
2 tablespoons Cointreau
1 cup whipping cream
Twisted lime slices
Stemmed maraschino cherries

Combine coconut and melted butter, tossing with a fork. Press over bottom and up sides of 9-inch glass pie plate. Bake at 300°F for 25 minutes or until golden brown. Set aside to cool.

Meanwhile, add water to pineapple syrup to make 1-1/2 cups liquid. Sprinkle gelatin over liquid in a small saucepan; stir in sugar, salt, lime zest, and juice. Heat mixture to boiling, stirring constantly until sugar dissolves; remove from heat. Beat egg yolks until foamy; gradually pour mixture over eggs, beating constantly. Stir in rum and Cointreau. Chill mixture 30 to 40 minutes until consistency of unbeaten egg white. Beat egg white until stiff peaks form. Fold into gelatin mixture until well blended. Whip cream until stiff. Fold cream and pineapple into gelatin mixture. Turn into coconut pie shell. Chill at least 2 to 3 hours before serving. Garnish with twisted lime slices and cherries before serving.

Pineapple Fruitcake

Makes 2 loaves

Though we think of fruitcakes at Christmas, this one can be enjoyed year 'round.

1 package (18-1/4 ounces) yellow cake mix
1/2 cup crushed pineapple
4 eggs
1 teaspoon salt
1 tablespoon lemon extract
2 cups raisins
1/2 pound candied pineapple, cut in narrow strips
1/2 pound whole red candied cherries
2 to 3 cups coarsely chopped macadamia nuts
3/4 cup flour

Combine yellow cake mix, pineapple, eggs, salt, and lemon extract; beat until smooth and creamy. Combine fruits and nuts; mix well with flour; stir into batter. Line two 8 × 4 × 3-inch loaf pans with triple thicknesses of waxed paper. Grease paper well. Pour batter into pans. Bake at 275°F for 2 hours and 45 minutes or until wooden pick inserted comes out clean. Cool before storing or wrapping.

Ginger-Pineapple Torte

Serves 8–10

*This delicious torte is easy to make and can be made in advance
and refrigerated until ready to serve.*

1 can (1-1/4 pounds) crushed pineapple, drained, reserving 1/2
    cup syrup
1 package (14-1/2 ounces) gingerbread mix
1/2 cup dairy sour cream
1 large banana, sliced
2 tablespoons lemon juice
1 cup whipping cream
1/4 cup powdered sugar
1 teaspoon vanilla
1/2 cup chopped macadamia nuts

Blend 1/2 cup pineapple syrup into gingerbread mix. Beat in
sour cream and pour into two greased, 8-inch round cake pans.
Bake at 350°F for 20 to 25 minutes or until wooden pick inserted in center comes out clean. Turn out onto wire racks to cool.
Meanwhile, combine banana with lemon juice in small bowl;
toss to coat banana slices completely. Whip cream with powdered sugar and vanilla until stiff peaks form. Place one layer
gingerbread on cake plate; spread with one-half of whipped
cream. Arrange banana slices around edge. Top with remaining gingerbread layer; spread with remaining whipped cream.
Sprinkle nuts around edge and spoon pineapple in center.

Easy Pineapple Sorbet

Serves about 6

Cool and refreshing. Additional chunks of pineapple may be folded in before freezing for extra crunch and texture.

1 medium fresh pineapple, peeled and cut into chunks
1 cup sugar
3 tablespoons fresh lemon juice

Combine all ingredients in blender or food processor container; cover and blend until smooth. Pour into a shallow pan; freeze until firm. Return to blender or food processor; blend until smooth again. Pour into pan and freeze again.

TIP

To measure granulated sugar, dip nested measuring cup into sugar and level top of cup.

To measure brown sugar, pack into nested measuring cup and level top of cup. Sugar should hold its shape when removed from cup.

Pineapple Cloud Dessert

Serves about 12

This light dessert is silken in texture. It simply melts in your mouth!

4 extra-large egg yolks
1/2 cup sugar
1/8 teaspoon salt
1-1/2 tablespoons dark Jamaican rum, optional
2 (8-ounce) packages cream cheese, softened
1 can (8-1/4 ounces) crushed pineapple, drained
1 teaspoon lemon zest
1 cup whipping cream, whipped
Semi-sweet chocolate curls

Beat egg yolks with sugar, salt, and rum until thick and creamy. Add cheese and beat until smooth and light. Fold pineapple and lemon zest into cheese mixture; spoon into stemmed sherbet glasses. Chill 2 or more hours or until set. Garnish with whipped cream; sprinkle with chocolate curls to serve.

TIP

Chocolate will keep for a year at room temperature. It is best to keep it stored below 70°F.

Pineapple Chiffon Cake

Serves about 16

You'll enjoy this light and delicate cake served plain or with ice cream.

2-1/4 cups flour
1-1/2 cups sugar
1 tablespoon baking powder
1 teaspoon salt
1/2 cup canola oil
7 eggs, separated
1 can (8-1/4 ounces) crushed pineapple
1 teaspoon lemon zest
1 tablespoon fresh lemon juice
2 tablespoons water
1 teaspoon vanilla
1/2 teaspoon cream of tartar

Combine flour with 1 cup sugar, baking powder, and salt in mixing bowl. Make a "well" in center of dry ingredients and add oil, egg yolks, pineapple with all syrup, lemon zest and juice, water, and vanilla. Beat until mixture is well blended. Beat egg whites with cream of tartar in large mixing bowl until soft peaks form. Slowly beat in remaining 1/2 cup sugar, continuing to beat until stiff peaks form. Pour pineapple mixture slowly over entire surface of egg whites, gently cutting and folding in with rubber spatula until completely blended. Turn into ungreased 10-inch tube pan. Bake on lowest oven rack at 325°F for 60 to 70 minutes or until wooden pick inserted in cake comes out clean. Invert and let "hang" until cooled. Frost as desired or serve plain with scoop of ice cream.

Pineapple Meringue Pie

Serves 8–10

This classic, delicately flavored pineapple pie is topped "mile high" with meringue.

1 can (1-1/4 pounds) crushed pineapple
1-1/2 cups sugar
1/2 cup water
1/3 cup cornstarch
2 tablespoons dry sherry, optional
1 tablespoon lemon zest
1/4 teaspoon salt
4 eggs, separated
2 tablespoons butter
1 (9-inch) baked pastry shell
1/4 teaspoon cream of tartar

Combine pineapple with all syrup, 1 cup sugar, water, cornstarch, sherry, lemon zest, and salt in saucepan; stir well to combine. Heat to boiling, stirring constantly until mixture boils and thickens enough so that spoon leaves trail when drawn through mixture; remove from heat. Beat a little hot mixture into egg yolks. Return to hot mixture and cook, stirring constantly, 1 to 2 minutes longer over low heat. Stir in butter and pour at once into pastry shell. Beat egg whites with cream of tartar until soft peaks form. Beat in remaining

1/2 cup sugar, gradually adding 2 tablespoons at a time, until stiff peaks form. Spread over warm filling, sealing edge of crust. Bake at 400°F for 7 to 10 minutes or until golden brown. Cool completely, about 1 hour, before serving.

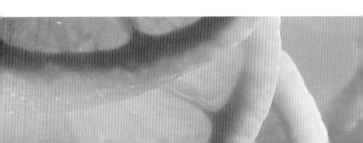

Soufflé Cointreau

Serves 6–8

*Serve a lovely, spectacular light soufflé. Fail-safe, too,
if the directions are followed exactly.*

1 (1-1/4 pounds) crushed pineapple, drained, reserving syrup
1 tablespoon Cointreau
2 tablespoons cornstarch
3/4 cup milk
1-1/2 tablespoons butter
3 whole eggs
1 egg white
1/2 teaspoon cream of tartar
1/4 teaspoon salt
1/4 cup sugar
Sugar for top of soufflé
Cointreau sauce (recipe follows)

Combine 1 cup pineapple with Cointreau; warm gently; set
aside. Butter 5-cup soufflé dish. Fold a 25-inch length of foil
6-inches wide in half to make a 3-inch-wide strip; fasten
around top of dish, using a paper clip where foil overlaps.
Secure with string around outside of dish so sides of dish are
built up. Butter inside of collar.

Stir cornstarch into milk in small saucepan; add butter and heat to boiling over moderate heat, stirring constantly until mixture thickens and comes to a full boil; remove from heat. Separate whole eggs and beat yolks lightly; slowly stir hot milk mixture into yolks. Beat 4 egg whites with cream of tartar and salt until soft peaks form. Gradually beat in sugar, beating until stiff meringue forms. Fold 1/4 of meringue into egg yolk mixture thoroughly, add remaining meringue and fold in quickly. Pour warm crushed pineapple and Cointreau into prepared dish. Spoon soufflé mixture into dish; sprinkle top lightly with sugar. Set dish in shallow pan with about 1 inch hot water. Place on lowest oven shelf. Bake at 375°F for 30 minutes; turn heat down to 350°F and bake additional 20 minutes or until set. Remove collar carefully and serve immediately with Cointreau Sauce from soufflé dish.

Cointreau Sauce: Stir 2 teaspoons cornstarch into reserved crushed pineapple and syrup; add 1 tablespoon dark corn syrup, 1 tablespoon butter, and dash of salt. Heat to boiling, stirring constantly. Remove from heat and stir in 1/4 cup Cointreau. Serve warm. *Yield*: About 1-1/2 cups sauce.

Pineapple Fruit Cup

Serves about 6–8

Here's a nice, light dessert that will go well with any menu.

1 can (1-1/4 pounds) pineapple chunks, drained, reserving
   1/2 cup syrup
1 can (11 ounces) mandarin oranges, drained
1/2 cup sliced dates
1 red apple
1 fresh pear
1 banana, sliced
1 tablespoon honey
1 teaspoon lime zest
1 tablespoon lime juice
Toasted sweetened coconut flakes

Combine pineapple, oranges, and dates in a deep glass bowl.
Core apple and pear, leaving skins on; cut into bite-size
chunks. Toss apple, pear, and banana with pineapple mixture.
Blend honey, lime zest, and juice into reserved pineapple
syrup; pour over fruits, tossing lightly. Chill well. Top with
toasted coconut flakes to serve.

PRESERVES

Sterilizing Glasses, Sealing, and Storing for Preserves:

Sterilize glass by:

1. Placing clean glasses upside down in hot water; bring water to a boil and continue boiling 10 to 15 minutes OR
2. Placing glasses in pressure cooker or pressure saucepan, exhaust air, and bring to 5 pounds pressure. Turn off heat and wait until pointer returns to zero before opening.

After sterilization, hot glasses should be drained, not wiped. Sterilize covers by placing them in boiling water 2 to 3 minutes

Sealing and Storing:

As soon as jelly is cooked, pour into hot, sterilized glasses, filling them to within 1/2 inch of the top. Cover immediately with a thin layer of hot melted paraffin. When the jelly is cold, seal by adding another layer of melted paraffin (about 1/8-inch thick); tip glass and allow paraffin to run around edges in order to ensure perfect seal. Cut a piece of string about 1 inch longer than diameter of jar and place on top of first layer of paraffin before the second layer is poured onto it. This helps in removal of the paraffin.

When paraffin is firmly set, wipe glasses with damp cloth; cover with lids. Label and store in a cool, dry, dark place.

Caution: Take great care in melting paraffin as it is highly flammable. Heat it slowly and remove from burner when melted. If possible, melt paraffin over hot water as recommended by the manufacturer.

Pineapple-Apricot Conserve

Makes about 1-1/2 quarts

*This conserve makes a wonderful gift, especially
if poured into attractive jars.*

1 pound dried apricots
1-1/2 cups water
3 medium oranges
2 tablespoons orange zest
1 can (1-1/4 pounds) crushed pineapple
3 cups sugar

Hot paraffin wax for sealing

Combine apricots with water; simmer, uncovered, 15 minutes
or until apricots are soft and most of the water is absorbed;
set aside. Grate peel from oranges to make 3 tablespoons
orange zest; peel oranges, removing all the white membrane.
Cut oranges in fourths; remove seeds. Combine apricots and
orange pieces in blender and purée; pour into large pot and
add undrained pineapple, orange zest, and sugar. Simmer
over low heat until thickened, about 5 to 7 minutes, stirring
constantly. Pour into hot, sterilized jars and seal with paraffin.
Allow paraffin to cool before covering with lid.

Pineapple Jam

Makes about 2 quarts

Delicious on toasted bread or as filling for cookies.

12 cups chopped fresh pineapple
6 cups sugar
1/3 cup lemon juice
Rind of 2 lemons, sliced in thin 1/2-inch strips

Hot paraffin wax for sealing

Combine pineapple with sugar and let stand overnight in refrigerator. Add lemon juice and rind; cook over low heat for about 2 hours or until thickened. Pour into hot, sterilized jars and seal with paraffin. Allow paraffin to cool before covering with lid.

NOTE

Firm-ripe or under-ripe fruit should be used for jelly. Pectin and acid content decrease as the fruit ripens. Use overripe fruits for butter, jam, or marmalade.

Pineapple Jelly
Makes about 8 (8-ounce) jars

This easy-to-make jelly reminds me of fine marmalade.

1 lime
1 can (6 ounces) frozen concentrated pineapple juice
1 can frozen concentrated pineapple-grapefruit* juice
1 package (1-3/4 ounces) dry pectin
2-1/2 cups water
5-1/2 cups sugar
1/4 teaspoon ground ginger

Hot paraffin wax for sealing

Pare peel of lime very thinly, being careful not to get any
white layer of rind; cut into very thin 1-inch slivers; set aside.
Squeeze juice and reserve. Combine frozen juices with pectin
and water in large saucepan; cook over medium-high heat,
stirring constantly, until bubbles form around the edge. Add
sugar, ginger, lime peel, and lime juice all at once; bring to
a full rolling boil. Boil 1 minute, stirring constantly. Remove
from heat; skim. Pour into sterilized 8-ounce jelly jars.
Seal with hot paraffin. Allow paraffin to cool before covering
with lid.

*May use frozen concentrated pineapple-orange juice instead.

Chunky Pineapple Chutney

Makes about 3 quarts

Try this delicious chutney with your curry—the chunky pieces of pineapple give this chutney an interesting texture. The quality and flavor will improve after 2 to 3 months in storage.

3 cans (1-1/4 pounds each) pineapple chunks
4 cups brown sugar, packed
3 cups cider vinegar
1 clove garlic, finely chopped
1 package (15 ounces) raisins
1 package (11 ounces) currants
1 pound chopped macadamia nuts
2 tablespoons fresh or crystallized ginger root
2 tablespoons instant minced onion
1 tablespoon orange zest
1-1/2 teaspoons salt
1 teaspoon ground allspice
1 teaspoon ground cinnamon
2 small chopped red peppers, seeded
1/4 teaspoon nutmeg

Hot paraffin wax for sealing

Combine all ingredients in a large saucepan or kettle; stir to mix well. Bring to a boil; cook over medium heat, stirring frequently to prevent scorching, one hour or until thickened and of desired consistency. Pour boiling hot chutney into hot, sterilized jars and seal at once with paraffin. Allow paraffin to cool before covering with lid. Serve with meats and curried dishes.

63

Pineapple-Papaya Marmalade

Makes about 1-1/2 pints

This delicious marmalade is an excellent recipe to use an abundance of pineapple and papaya.

2 cups diced fresh ripe pineapple
2 cups diced ripe papaya
1 quart sugar
2 teaspoons lemon zest
1/2 cup fresh lemon juice

Combine pineapple and sugar in large shallow saucepan; stir to mix well and let stand while preparing papaya. Add lemon zest and juice. Bring mixture to boiling point slowly over medium-low heat; cook about 30 minutes or until mixture sheets from spoon or until temperature on a candy thermometer reaches 224°F. Pour immediately into hot, sterilized 8-ounce jars and seal with hot paraffin. Allow paraffin to cool before covering with lid.

NOTE

This marmalade expires after 6 months.

BEVERAGES

Pineapple Juice

Makes about 2-1/2 to 3 quarts

*Nothing is as refreshing as fresh pineapple juice.
It is worth the extra effort.*

1 fresh pineapple

Cut and peel ripe pineapple into 8 to 10 lengthwise pieces and then into 1-inch cubes. Squeeze the fruit through poi cloth or sugar sack to extract the juice. Chill and serve.

Pineapple Punch

Serves about 6

A refreshing beverage on a hot summer day.

3/4 cup sugar
3/4 cup water
4 cups fresh pineapple juice
3/4 cup orange juice
1/2 cup fresh lemon juice
1 teaspoon finely chopped mint leaves

Dissolve sugar in water; combine with fruit juices and mint; mix well. Pour over cracked ice to serve.

Hawaiian Fruit Punch

Makes about 74 4-ounce servings

*The refreshing pineapple flavor is paired with
orange juice for this popular drink.*

1 can (12 ounces) frozen lemonade, thawed
1 can (46 ounces) fruit punch
2 cans (46-ounces each) pineapple juice
3 cans (46-ounces each) orange juice
1 bottle (28 ounces) lemon-lime soda
Chopped mint leaves

Chill all ingredients well. Just before serving, combine all
ingredients in a large punchbowl and serve over crushed ice.

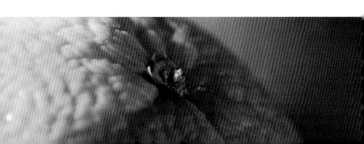

Guava-Pineapple Punch

Makes about 12 4-ounce servings

Looking for a simple beverage recipe? Here's one that you must try.

1 can (46 ounces) pineapple juice, chilled
1 can (46 ounces) guava juice, chilled
1 bottle (28 ounces) ginger ale, chilled
1 quart pineapple sherbet

Combine pineapple and guava juices in large punch bowl; mix well. Just before serving, add ginger ale and sherbet. Serve over ice.

Pineapple Shake

Makes about 3 cups

Shakes and smoothies are the beverages of choice for many. You'll enjoy the flavor of this refreshing pineapple-banana combo.

1 can (12 ounces) pineapple juice
1 medium banana, sliced
1 pint vanilla ice cream

Combine all ingredients in a blender; blend until smooth.

Pink Champagne Punch

Makes about 16 4-ounce servings

This is an excellent beverage to serve at an afternoon reception.

1 can (46 ounces) pineapple-pink grapefruit juice drink
1/2 cup sugar
1/2 teaspoon Angostura bitters
1/4 cup brandy
1/5 bottle pink champagne
Ice cubes

All ingredients should be well chilled. Combine pineapple-pink grapefruit juice drink, sugar, bitters, and brandy in large punch bowl. Add champagne and ice just before serving.

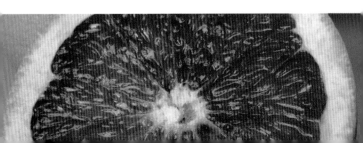

Fruity Slush

Makes about 23 4-ounce servings

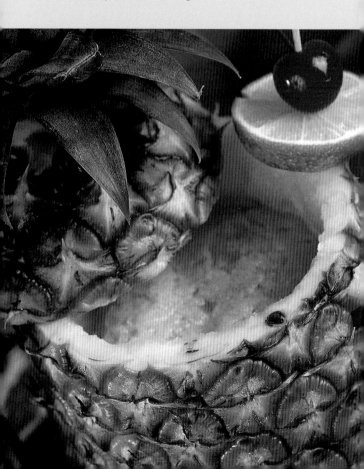

A most refreshing treat, especially during the hot summer months.

1 cup sugar
2-3/4 cups water
2 ripe medium bananas, chopped
3 cups unsweetened pineapple juice
1 can (6 ounces) frozen orange juice concentrate
3 tablespoons lemon juice
1 (1-liter) bottle carbonated water or lemon-lime carbonated
      beverage, chilled

Stir together sugar and water until sugar dissolves. In a blender
jar, combine bananas, 1-1/2 cups pineapple juice and orange juice
concentrate; cover and blend until smooth. Add to sugar mixture.
Stir in remaining pineapple juice and lemon juice. Pour into
13 × 9 × 2-inch baking pan. Freeze for several hours or until firm.

To serve, let mixture stand at room temperature 20 to 30 minutes. To form slush, scrape large spoon across surface of the
frozen mixture; spoon into a punch bowl. Slowly pour carbonated water down the side of the bowl; stir gently to mix.

VARIATION: Spiked Slushy Punch

Add 1-1/2 cups rum or vodka with lemon juice to recipe.
Allow frozen mixture to stand at room temperature 5 to
10 minutes before scraping with spoon to form slush.
Yield: About 26 (4-ounce) servings.

NOTE

For individual serving, combine equal amounts of slush
and carbonated water; stir to mix.

Pineapple Nog

Serves 3

Start the day with this delicious nog.

1 can (6 ounces) frozen pineapple-orange juice* concentrate
3 eggs, slightly beaten
Nutmeg

Reconstitute juice with water as directed on can; blend well.
Combine 1 cup juice with 1 egg in blender; blend until frothy.
Top with nutmeg to serve. Repeat twice again to use all eggs.

*Use any frozen juice concentrate of choice. If sweeter nog is
desired, add 1 tablespoon honey for each egg.

TIP

Most manufacturers and merchants agree that whole and
ground spices have a two-year shelf life once opened.
Best stored away from heat.

APPENDICES

Ways to Cut Fresh Pineapple

PINEAPPLE BASKET

1. Make a vertical cut to the core a little to the right of center. Do the same a little left of center to form handle. Remove fruit from under handle.
2. Remove rind from fruit pieces removed from sides and cut into wedges.
3. Cut out fruit from basket using a curved knife. Slice into wedges. Fill basket.

WEDGES AND SPEARS

1. Cut top and bottom of pineapple off. Remove rind from pineapple by cutting strips of rind away.
2. Remove "eyes" from the fruit by cutting away diagonal strips.
3. Cut into wedges or spears.

QUARTERS

1. Cut pineapple from bottom through crown, first in half, then in quarters.
2. Cut away core, leaving crown on.
3. Loosen fruit by cutting close to rind with sharp knife.
4. Cut crosswise through loosened fruit; cut lengthwise into bite-size pieces.

LŪʻAU STYLE

1. Cut top and bottom of pineapple away, saving bottom and crown.
2. Remove center of pineapple and slice into spears.
3. Replace pineapple spears into shell.
4. Replace bottom and crown of pineapple so that it looks "uncut."

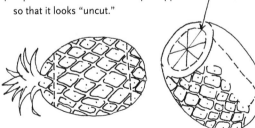

OUTRIGGER

1. Cut pineapple into quarters, leaving crown on.
2. Loosen fruit by cutting under the core but without removing it. Also cut close to rind.
3. Remove fruit and cut crosswise.
4. Replace fruit into shell in staggered arrangement.

Glossary

B

Bean Sprouts:
Fresh or canned sprouted mung beans.

C

Chinese Parsley:
Leaves of the coriander plant. Also called cilantro.

Chinese Black Beans:
Soybeans fermented in salt, garlic, and other spices.

Chives:
Related to the onion and leek, this fragrant herb has slender, vivid green, hollow stems. Chives have a mild onion flavor and are available fresh year-round.

Chutney:
A spicy relish made of fruits, spices, and herbs. Often used as a condiment with curry or glaze for meat.

Coconut:
The fruit of the coconut tree featuring a hard brown outer shell and containing white meat on the inside. The liquid extracted from shredded coconut meat can be drunk as milk or used in cooking.

E

Ehu:
Hawaiian name for red snapper, delicate and sumptuous; lesser known than 'ōpakapaka.

G

Ginger:
A brown, fibrous, knobby rhizome that keeps for long periods of time. To use, peel the brown skin and slice, chop, or puree.

Guava:
A round tropical fruit with a yellow skin and pink inner flesh and many seeds. Grown commercially in Hawai'i. The puree or juice is available as a frozen concentrate. Guava can also be made into jams, jellies, and sauces.

M

Macadamia Nuts:
A rich, oily nut grown mostly on the Big Island of Hawai'i. Also called "mac nuts."

Mango:
Gold and green tropical fruit available in many supermarkets. Available fresh June through September in Hawai'i.

O

'Ōpakapaka:
A blue snapper with a delicate flavor. Good poached, baked, or sautéed. Substitute any red snapper, sea bass, or monkfish.

P

Papaya:
The most common papaya used in Hawai'i is the solo papaya, a tropical fruit with a yellow flesh, black seeds, and a perfumey scent. Other types are larger and may have pink flesh; all are suitable for island recipes.

Poi cloth:
Used to strain poi. Substitute with a double thickness of cheese cloth.

S

Soy Sauce:
A dark, salty liquid made from soybeans, flour, salt, and water. Dark soy sauce is stronger than light soy sauce. A staple in most Asian cuisines. Also called *shoyu*.

U

Uhu:
Hawaiian name for parrotfish, usually served steamed, Chinese-style.

Z

Zest:
The colored portion of a citrus fruit's rind. When removing the zest from a citrus fruit, it's important to avoid removing the bitter white pith just below the colored portion.